JOSEPH M. KINGS

The Holy Grind

Contents

Foreword — iv

Preface — vi

Acknowledgement — viii

1 Lesson from the Mill — 1

2 Sacrifice, Discipline and Focus — 4

3 An Apple Does Not Fall Far From The Tree — 8

4 The Breakthrough — 12

5 Fatherhood — 15

6 The Journey To Christ and Ministry — 17

7 Embarking on a New Journey — 21

8 Fame or Shame? — 24

9 The Turning Point — 26

10 Becoming Homeless — 29

11 The Shelter — 32

12 Waiting Upon The Lord — 36

13 In Search of A Solution — 39

14 Never Give Up — 42

15 Joy Comes in the Morning — 50

About the Author — 55

Foreword

It all started in the playground for me, that one-hour break time was a place where I'd exercise my business acumen. I'd sell sweets, chewing gum and crisps in exchange for money or dinner tickets. The dinner tickets would then be used to buy multiple burgers, drinks and doughnuts in the cafeteria to be resold during the next lesson. Looking back at the 12-year-old me, this was the start of my "Holy Grind" as Joseph quite rightly says in the title of this book.

I've sold various things since then from motorbikes to cars to jewellery and diamonds, one thing that I kept consistent throughout, is the relationship with people. That's what has now allowed me to realise why I'm in the field I am in today. As a publicist or PR to the elite, I manage the perception, communication and branding of the largest brands, businesses and high profile individuals in the world. Throughout life's adversities, I've never seen anything as a loss, I've always seen everything as a stepping stone to success.

This book gives the fundamentals of being an entrepreneur and life's ups and downs. It shows you that no matter what life throws at you, you must continue the course and stay persistent. It goes to show that business starts at home, rather than the classroom. The closest people around you have the most influence in your life and are prime examples of how you conduct yourself in the real world, therefore giving you a core understanding of good business ethics, in this case, we all have a "Grandma Kings" in our lives, some way or another.

Quincy Dash

Preface

"My Story is filled with broken pieces, terrible choices and ugly truths. It's also filled with a major Comeback, peace in my soul and it is Grace that saved my life"

Firstly it could be worse. Secondly, it could be a lot worse, but I must remember that the aforementioned is all about grinding. The question I always ask myself and tell myself is, IS IT WORTH IT? I want to live a fulfilling life. I want to do this, and Grinding is part of the deal.

"Nana Korobi Yaoki Jinsey Wa Kore Kara Da" Fall seven times, rise eight times life begins now. Grinding is being sent back down and never giving up, losing sight of the top. Being at your breaking point but keep knowing you can't quit.

As I was waiting and watching my Grandma's grinding mill 25 years ago, I wondered why I had to watch the process of transforming wheat into fine flour. I never enjoyed the noise or the dust in that environment, but I had to be there through it all. It took most of my playtime, although the result was magnificent. However, the process was painful. Grandma kept me in check, she always said to remain focused, but I never understood it at all till I faced my challenges 20 years later.

Even Grandma's advice and life lessons were not enough when I felt the cold, rain over me, with nowhere to go - then I realised I was homeless. I was never a big fan of McDonald's, but I fell in love with it as it became my hiding place because I had no source of income and I was in and out of the hospital due to a stroke. At times being in the hospital felt better because it was slightly warm and safe.

When you get hit by a few things at once, it affects your ability to think straight. You are firefighting all the time. Depression saps your energy as it makes it hard to get up in the morning and put a rational plan together, but hey, you just keep on Grinding. I look around at all those who have failed to get what they want, and I felt that I do not deserve to get what I wanted either. But the obstacles and suffering I endured, all the things I had given up that brought me to this.

The Grind Is On.

Acknowledgement

I would like to thank God Almighty in the process of putting this book together. He gave me strength and power to believe in my passion and purpose; I could never have done it without faith in Him. I would like to express my gratitude to many people who saw me through the journey of writing this book; to everyone who provided support and the guidance, especially to the Apostle of our generation, the late, Apostle Taffy Donzwa, a man who truly feared God. Dr Emmanuel Sanyika, for your support in finding me the best publishers and your spiritual guidance, I tip my hat to you, Sir. I'm grateful even for your inspiration. To Levi Stirling and family, you guys rock! You have been a pillar to us even in the time we had no roof over our heads, you sacrificed all and took us in thank you.

To the Manchester Shelter institute, I would like to extend my gratitude, and on behalf of those that are still homeless, we thank you for all you did for us and to what you continue to do for others, as you accommodated us and showed us love. To RM Publishers, thank you for your patience; you stood by me till we got the best results. You are the best. To my big brother Jacob, I can barely find the right words to express. You have always made me feel so proud to have you as my brother, and you bring the best out of me. Thank you for all your support, love and advice.

To my beautiful wife Florence, I am so thankful that I have you in my corner pushing me when I was ready to give up and for believing and staying by me through it all. You are the best and remember this, in the walk of fame of my life, you are the only star. You are the only support I have and ever needed. I love you.

If there is anyone I forgot to mention by name, please do not hold it against me. I thank you and much love to you all.

1

Lesson from the Mill

During the summer of '92, there I was at my Grandma's house. Every time I visited her, I would go and help her out at the mill. Being a young boy, I was full of energy - wanting to spend time with my friends - although this wasn't always the case - as I had to be at the mill helping out. I had one of the most unique experiences of my life. As a young boy, I kept losing focus because of too many distractions. My mind was thinking of playing yet I had an assignment to keep an eye on the mill. This led to the mill breaking down so often, and it meant that I had to spend more time working at the mill rather than to be with my friends.

Grandma would always say, "You're delaying yourself, concentrate for a few hours, and then you can be with your friends." But I did not take hid to her advice. In life, we tend to start something, whether it is a business, a relationship or a project. Yet, we find ourselves taking longer or even quitting due to pressure, obstacles and distractions.

We lose the ability to focus as distractions become a habit.

We tend to want to do everything at once and at the end we achieve nothing. As an entrepreneur, you will have a lot on your plate. Staying on track can be a challenge with consistent demands, dealing with phone calls, clients and even personal issues. While multitasking is an important skill, there's also a downside to it because it reduces our intelligence as we are prone to making mistakes.

It took me time to realise that every time I lost focus at the mill, there was a stoppage that meant my playtime was cut short. I had to walk a long distance back to the main house to get my uncle to come and fix the machine. It took most of my "me time" and this meant I had to stay there longer than expected. I remember the late nights I had to stay at the mill, and by the time I went back home, my friends would have gone. I then realized that if I didn't pay attention, the machine would keep breaking down, and this meant I lost my "me time." I understood what made me lose focus in the first place. I was always thinking about going out to play.

Over the years, I've realized that if you harness your determination and stay focused by setting up your day the night before, it does help. I used to say, I will do it later, and that was procrastination - a clear sign of failure.
   Always do the most difficult things first and eliminate distractions and time-wasters. Feeling overwhelmed is directly related to a sense of control. As soon as you think you're losing control over your time, relationships or life in general your responsibilities feel like burdens piling up on your shoulders.

You then feel anxious and you cannot do everything or appear resentful about the expectations people have for you. When that happens, always review the choices that led to being overwhelmed, get your priorities back in check. Ask yourself why you're doing the task. Back to the mill story, my purpose was to please my Grandma, and because I loved her so dearly, I would do anything for her even if it meant sacrificing my playtime. My Grandma always encouraged me to set goals and work hard to achieve them. I remember her saying to me one time, "Don't be a follower and don't set limits on what you can achieve."

My Grandma was known for her baking. The cakes that she made were the best in town; even my friends loved them. I guess most of them were my friends because of the cakes. Most times, we love the glory but not the pain. For every glory, there's a story. As time elapsed, I began to enjoy being at the mill mainly cause of the results.

"In life, choose what you love, be it a job, and you will never have to work a day in your life," according to Warren Buffet. I fell in love with the mill, and I even made my friends come and keep me company, I hope it wasn't because of the cakes!

2

Sacrifice, Discipline and Focus

Growing up, we tend to have wise elders in our lives. Early in my life, I encountered knowledgeable people who seemed to know something about life. My Grandma was a blessing to me, and I cannot hope to have any other person as beautiful and adorable as her. Grandma's garden was grown with seeds of love and warm sunshine. It was sprinkled, now and then, with a rain shower and sown with gentle and loving hands. During my time at Grandma's, I learnt so much, although at the time, I never thought it was that important.

Only years later, I realised how important it was. Grandma always said, "Be disciplined JOJO" that's what she called me. "Self-discipline is key JOJO." I would still laugh it off and say, "Ok, Granny, I will." My Grandma was full of wisdom. She could see through me, and she knew I was not listening though however, she never gave up on me.

Self-discipline is a pattern of behaviour where we choose to do what we know we should do, rather than what we want to do. As a young boy, I always wanted to be with my friends and play. I remember at one time I tried to rush the process of the mill by overfilling the hub thinking the more I put, the quicker I would finish, but the hub was not having any of that. This action caused it to have a stoppage, and I delayed myself even further. No matter what I did, all the tricks I tried, I still had to go back to the mill until it completed.

Self-discipline is the inner power that pushes you to get out of bed to exercise rather than to sleep-in. It is the assentation of will power over basic desires and is synonymous with self-control. It gives you the strength to withstand hardships and difficulties, whether physical, emotional, mental and spiritual. It allows you not to go for immediate satisfaction to gain something better, and it requires time and effort. After mastering the principle of discipline, I enjoyed every moment at the mill.

Discipline is one of the most if not the cornerstone to living a successful and fulfilling life, something we should strive to master. In life, we tend to opt for short cuts as for some; it's not time-consuming. Short cuts have never paid as many a time we tend to meet up with unexpected obstacle's that can be overwhelming. In most cases, we give up. I tried several times, but if my Grandma's mill would speak, I suppose it would write a syllabus about what I made it go through all because of lack of discipline.

Life is a journey that has hurdles along the way. Challenges make us stronger as we overcome them. In life, there will be setbacks. As my Grandma would say, "Every setback is a set up for a comeback." Imagine if Colonel Saunders, the founder of Kentucky Fried Chicken had given up on his vision, we wouldn't be enjoying those bargain buckets or those drive-throughs. Considering the number of hurdles he encountered, giving up was not an option. I always wondered what his secret was, but my Grandma's advice about discipline, determination and focus would come to my mind. Today we celebrate the lives of great people that have excelled in their fields of expertise, and we admire their lifestyles, but sometimes we are not willing to go through the preparations and obstacles they've had to face.

We often opt for the easy way out or "short cuts." I was looking at one of the greatest, and fastest Man celebrated worldwide; a decorated athlete, Usain Bolt, the fastest sprinter ever. He holds records both in 100 and 200 meters and is also known as the Lightning Bolt. It would take him at least a full year in most cases, even longer, to prepare himself just to run less than 10 seconds. And today he is who he is because of sacrifice, discipline and focus.

Looking at people who tend to take short cuts, they end up grounded to zero due to "Quick Fixes" for example taking drugs or cheating. Most businesses are failing due to these so-called "short cuts" and having shaky foundations. Every short cut is an adjustment to your success. The power of old habits is strong; even if there are newer, faster and seem better. The lack of understanding; be it a problem or solution, leads many to assume they have found a short cut falsely. Short cuts can be based on laziness leading to avoidance of effort being ingrained in many people. We often don't look for the best answer or way but rather the lowest effort we can get by.

Discipline means focus under control. It's motivating on its own. Every time you aim for the moon and miss, discipline tells you not to worry but to stay focused; at least we can see the stars. Lack of discipline, on the other hand, tells you to forget it, to quit, you're wasting your time, and you'll never make it. At times you find yourself surrounded by people who only know failure, people that never made it, people who gave up.

Discipline and focus will speak louder to overshadow all these other voices and say what if it works; others have proven it is possible like Obama would say, "YES WE CAN."

3

An Apple Does Not Fall Far From The Tree

I grew up within a business-oriented family, and I resonate well with the saying, "An Apple doesn't fall far from the tree." Most of us inherit our parents' characteristics. I come from a family of seven; two girls and five boys. I'm the youngest of the boys, and I had a lot to learn from my brothers. My parents had it all together business-wise, we were doing great owning superstores, tailoring shops, markets, properties and vehicles.

I believe my parents got some serious advice from my Grandma due to her accomplishments. Discipline, focus and determination played a significantly vital role. One thing I remember growing up was that our parents never took us shopping for anything except for school uniforms. We had a personal tailor that made us clothes, and we got food from the stores. It was great as everyone admired our family. During most holidays or some weekends, we would go to the shop to help out with the family business.

My older brother, Dominic, was eager as he was regarded as the clever one, growing up. Every time we got our school reports, he would make so much noise in the house to draw attention because of his good grades. And as for me I just enjoyed going to the shop to play video games or go to Grandma's.

We started to learn about business at a very young age. It did not make sense at the time as we just regarded it a family thing. The bookkeeping, counting of tills and stock-taking was part of accounting lessons we were learning for our tomorrow. One day, I remember we didn't go to the shop as it was a sports weekend at school. We had to be at school, and the parents had gone to work, as usual, leaving us behind. I remember how my brother and I learned how to drive. We came back from school early and decided to drive as we had a few cars around. The funny part was that both of us were short and we couldn't even reach for the paddles properly without the support of cushions.

We made a plan and got the cushions in place, called our friends over and the housemaids to help us accomplish our "mission impossible". My brother went on first. On this occasion, I was the cleverer one in case anything went wrong; I will be the one making noise when the parents came back. We got my brother in, and we all pushed him as he was learning the basics of controlling the vehicle. Mind you; we did not turn on the engine. It was too scary and exciting at the same time. It was our secret for some time as we continued to learn how to control the car but never turning on the engine.

One weekend our uncle came over to visit, and he brought his car and asked us if we could clean it for him. He gave us his keys, as he wanted the inside cleaned as well. He asked us if we could drive and before he could finish asking my brother had keys in his hands already. He asked us to move the car as soon as we finished cleaning it. The car was clean in no time, and my brother decided to go first. He started the car, and off he went, the rest is history. I remember my uncle came out screaming, shouting "Stop! Stop!" as my brother raved the vehicle as if it was going to blow up, and it was in first gear as we had never learned about gears.

It was a different ball game altogether. Finally, he was forced to stop with some obstacle by default, and I never had a chance to go as well, I was devastated. My parents heard about, but we never got into trouble as we had permission from our uncle and that was the last time I saw my parents leaving any car keys hanging around the house.

Our weekends carried on as usual, and on other holidays we would be at the shop. It was becoming more intense; the older we got, the more the responsibilities. It was sincerely proper training. During all this time, I kept thinking about my Grandma's advice as it was making more sense. I realised that nothing comes easy considering the hurdles and challenges that my parents had faced to where they were.

Discipline, determination and focus was the ultimate foundation. Years later, my other two older brothers broke away from the family business. They started their businesses. That was mind-blowing for me. Grandma's principles played a role in their lives as they remained focused and were determined not to fail at all costs. They were doing well in their line of business and made our parents proud. Finally, I finished my education studies but didn't want to look for work, not because I was lazy, but because of my upbringing - I always wanted to be my own boss.

My other brother, Jacob, relocated to the United States, which was a blow for me as he was my best friend. By this time, both parents had passed on, and the pressure was now mounting on me. I tried almost everything I knew, but nothing seemed to be working out for me.I kept grinding until an opportunity arose. An old friend from the neighbourhood approached me with a business proposal, and we set down to discuss all the nitty-gritty. We then finalised everything after we came to an agreement and opened a printing company.

4

The Breakthrough

In the first few months, we struggled by not having enough clients to maintain the business. However, we kept grinding, as Grandma would say. We then landed on a good contract that was life-changing. We got so busy that we even forgot that we ever struggled. We had contracts with schools printing t-shirts, posters, flyers and banners, and this opened more doors for us. We were doing so well that we even started employing people as we could not handle the workload.

I was ambitious, and I needed more. I was continually looking for something to invest in. I decided to team up with my elder brother in his business as he needed help due to much work. This was the game-changer as we made a lot of money and even forgot about the printing business. I also gave my friend my shares, but he decided to leave it and relocated to the United Kingdom. My new adventure required much travelling. Focus was the only thing that kept me there, not talking about the money.

We made so much money that we could afford drivers, but I never invested in anything. We splashed money everywhere, like Mayweather. As it kept coming in, we kept grinding. My brother in the United States rang me and said he wanted me to relocate and join him in the USA. As I was doing so well, I told him I would come only to visit and do some shopping. We made plans for me to visit him. The week before I was meant to go to the American Embassy, my friends and I went on a drinking spree as per our usual leisure. My elder brother was not impressed by my so-called new fast life which was full of activity, and often dangerous. We would go from nightclub to nightclub all weekend long without going home. We would buy new clothes every day to change, and bathing in hotels was the new lifestyle.

On a Sunday, a day before my appointment at the American Embassy, we decided to go home. The house was the only investment I had made at this point. I had managed to buy a farmhouse, including horses and farm equipment. We drank too much in that week, and as we drove home, my friend lost control of the vehicle, and we drove right under a bus. I don't even know how we managed to come out of it as the car was written off. People who saw the car would never have thought that there were people that survived in that.

I missed my appointment at the embassy as I was in the hospital. From that moment onward, things changed. I had an earnest talk with my elder brother the one I was doing business with, and he said to me if you don't change your way of living we will bury you sooner than you think. So he suggested I go away for a bit to gather myself together and by this time, I had missed my opportunity to go to the states.

I didn't stay long in the hospital. After a day, I was out as the doctors were on strike and made plans as soon as possible to take time off. The following weekend I was on the next plane to the United Kingdom. I was meant to be taking time off to re-focus and recover although for me it was a wake-up call at the same time. I then settled in the UK even though it was for a short time. I later received a call that my elder brother, my business partner, had passed away.

That was life changing and painful at the same time. It definitely changed the way I looked at life. As at that time I took life for granted. I then decided to settle in the UK although it was not easy. I was not used to the lifestyle and I never wanted to go to the UK in the first place. It was the worst experience having to find a job and work for somebody else.

5

Fatherhood

My first job was off-loading trucks, and that was painful, but I had to do it. I did the job for a while, and that was the same time my son, Nathan, was born. Things had to change as I now had responsibilities. I then met up with an old friend who had been in the Army and was back from his tour. We spent time together, drinking and doing everything that friends would do. We would spend almost every other weekend together as long as he was available. Months later, he then talked me into signing up to join him within the Army.

At first, I was adamant and hesitant. However, eventually, I saw myself signing up. I went for training and months later, I started enjoying the travelling and tours, even the training became part of my daily life. My son was now a few years older, and if I remember well, I was never around for him. I missed partly if not half of his early life; nursery days, the first day at school etc.

Years later, when my daughter Brianna was born, I realised that I didn't want to miss out on her early life too with the busy schedule of travelling and not being home all the time. This time around, I decided to make sacrifices not to miss every significant event in her life. I never missed her first day at school because I took her. We have a great father-daughter bond.

I remember once she had her first play at school and I was away in Donnington Barracks at work, but I had promised her that I would make it. I had to keep the promise and be there. Since I was at work, I had no time to change - I went straight to her school in my uniform. The moment she saw me, she started jumping about pointing to everyone I was her dad. That was an adorable moment to treasure. As I walked into the hall, the joy on her face said it all for me. Every other parents' day, I tried to be present to compensate for the years I missed on my son.

6

The Journey To Christ and Ministry

Years later, I got tired of my lifestyle. There was an emptiness, even though I had it all together, I knew something was missing. I decided to accept Christ as my Lord and Saviour. I surrendered my life to Him fully according to John 3:16 (NKJV), "For God so loved the world that he gave his one and only Son, that whoever believes in him shall not perish but have eternal life."

That was my turning point. I realised that God shows off with His Born Again children. I never lacked anything be it financially or emotionally as I had found inner joy and peace. The peace that the world peace keepers couldn't give. I started planning ahead now. I had to go back to the basics that my Grandma taught me.

My upbringing took a toll on my life. Whenever I was off from work, I would be up and about grinding. I would go to auctions buying stuff and re-selling. I was brought up in a business environment, so failure was not an option. Things began to take shape. The business started to produce results, and I never looked back. I was always driven, looking for more opportunities to invest in. As the business did well, I decided to set up a small store to test the waters though it was not easy. I almost closed the store at one point due to pressure. But I kept reminding myself that "every set back is a set up for a comeback."

I kept grinding day in day and day out. I didn't sleep much even though at this time, I had streams of income. I then embarked on another journey that was to further my education at Bolton University, and while I was there, I made contacts and decided to go into Television as well. I started working on a Talk Show. At this time, I had no social life per se, for anything I did had to do with business even my circles had to be in business or aspiring to be one way or another. The first year at University was not easy. The essays, the sleepless nights, the job and businesses was overwhelming.

As a born again child of God, there was a church I was attending for about two years. One Sunday, the Man of God there turned around in the middle of a sermon and said to me "You are called into Ministry." That was news to me as I never thought God would use someone like me. I then started to condemn myself and reflected on the sort of life I had lived before. I just brushed it aside and carried on as usual in the church as I was keen in the media department. It was a month later in church when he called me in the middle of the service and said leave that camera and rise as a Pastor. That was like a ton of bricks falling on my head. I didn't argue as I didn't know what even to say or question him as he had said God told him. I was speechless, and all I could do was obey the call and accepted the invitation.

Now the pressure was mounting on me, as I had so much going on. My work, school, businesses and was now a Pastor which meant I had to shepherd people which was time-consuming. I remember church was doing great growth-wise and the spiritual side as we did the best we could under the guidance of the Holy Spirit. There were some Sundays, I could not be in the church due to the nature of my Army job as it required for me to be travelling outside the country; be it for training or something else. I had an assistant Pastor that would take over during my absence.

As time went on, everything was going well in all aspects of my life. I remember the Man of God came over to our branch as we had a conference, and everyone there was excited about his visit. That very same day he fired me from being a Pastor due to a disagreement we had about the woman I wanted to marry. Even though he meant well, I was not marrying for him as it was my personal choice. So it sounded as if I was undermining his authority, but I had to stand my ground on this occasion. So he fired me.

Like any other company, if you get fired, you surrender the company's property, and at this time, the only thing in my possession was a vehicle he had given me to use. So he sent another Pastor to come and get it. I remember when the Pastor rang me and asked me to go to his place; I just drove straight to his home, not knowing the reason. I got there, and he explained that I had to surrender the car keys. It was a humiliating experience for me, but it never affected me as I had my businesses and was not on a salary, so really nothing changed.

I managed to get myself a taxi and paid for it when I got home as I had not carried enough money on me. After all the humiliation I went through, I kept my head up, and I never stopped attending church, because in the first place I did not come for men but for God. It was an awkward moment as many people kept addressing me as Pastor, but there had to be someone to correct them, more like someone was hired for just that reason, but then I realised it was out of envy.

7

Embarking on a New Journey

I kept doing what I knew best, grinding, and never looking back. I pursued my Talk Show which was my pride and joy—meeting up with celebrities and trying to get them on the show. My contact list grew from church leaders to musicians and footballers. I worked so hard to get the show aired on national TV. It was never easy; the number of doors that were closed on us, rejections we faced along the way, but we kept pushing. During this time, I was still attending church as usual as I kept reminding myself that I gave my life to God, not to man.

A year later, I had just left my office for the day, driving on my way home, I got a phone call but did not pick it as it was from one of the church Pastors. He kept calling me, and I did not answer. When I got home, after I had relaxed a bit, he decided to send me a text saying the Man of God wants to speak to me and asked me to pick up the phone. I asked myself so many questions as in what could be the issue be, what does he want? At least I knew for sure he could not fire me again, so I decided to pick the call after a while.

The first thing he said was, "How are you doing and how's business? Can you come to the house I need to see you?" I drove to his home, which was a bit of a distance, and as I got there, I was greeted as usual, but in my mind, I was still puzzled what could it be. I suspected maybe it had to do with my TV business as at this time I was spending most of my time with high profiled people. So much went through my head at the time. I then managed to see him, and we spoke then he said to me I want you to be my Personal Assistant.

Just him calling was humbling in itself and being his PA, and I was speechless. We spoke further, and I explained what I was doing as he had asked me how business was doing. At this time, I was nervous, still and anxious. Remembering just a year ago he fired me, and now he wanted me to be his PA yet people travelled from all over the country just to come to see him. Who was I to be his PA? At that moment, the first thing that I did was out of selfishness. I was like those that laughed at me before will dance to my music.

I didn't know what to say then, so I just said, "OK, thank you for the opportunity. I'm truly humbled." I was lost for words. It took me a few weeks for it to sink in. The time came for me to embark on my new journey. Although it was exciting, it required sacrificing at the same time. I left everything, including my businesses, my home and work, even dropped out of University as most of the time I would be out of the country. This was the ultimate sacrifice as there are many ways to be brave in this world. Sometimes bravery involves laying down your life for something bigger than you or someone else. At this time, it meant giving up everything I had ever achieved or everyone I loved, for the sake of ministry.

Travelling was never an issue for me as I was used to it while I was in the forces. The only difference was the conditions of where we would go and sleep. It was a different ball game. I stayed in the best hotels in the world. Dubai was more like a second home. I experienced so much with the Man of God. I met great servants of God. It was more like a dream. Bumping into celebrities was a daily occurrence, although I was used to it from my TV Show-business.

I was truly humbled to serve under such a Man of God, considering I drove the best cars I could ever imagine and ate from the best places. I remember at one time my family and friends would send me messages saying we have seen you have just checked in at the airport where next are you off to? Many times we would just come back to change bags, and we would be on the next flight the following day. I served faithfully, as it was an honour to help a man that was preaching the gospel of our Lord Jesus.

8

Fame or Shame?

At one time we had just landed in South Africa for a conference and the number of people that came to greet me was unbelievable, but little did I know they had been watching me on TV. At this time, I had become "famous" due to the programme that the Man of God entrusted me to present, and that was a humbling experience. All travel and accommodation were catered for, even the flights. I cannot recall all the countries I've been to, but I can tell of the countries I've never been to before. During my time, I've seen lives transformed, people healed, receiving Christ, and for me, that was the highlight of it all.

I was having the best time of my life until one day it dawned on me as I set down and started to think about my own life and family. I was living the so-called life that everyone else admired, but I couldn't afford to look after my own family. If made me question God, asking if this was His will.

How was it possible to serve God, yet my family struggled? I took a hard decision, gathered myself together and approached the man of God and told him that I had served him faithfully, but it was now time for me to take my leave. I realised it was time to re-focus on what comes first in my life. I took a leap of faith to re-define my purpose. My life at this point was on stand-by, although the media portrayed a wrong image.

My family had to come first in this instance. I managed to leave the man of God in good faith and harmony without regrets as I had done my best to serve a Man of God. My only regret was closing my income streams at that time. I should have kept the business running although other things such as my job and education, I had no option but to abandon. I rang my brother in the USA to tell him about the decision. He was disappointed that I had dropped everything in the first place. I moved back to the city we lived in with his help. Although moving from country to country with the man of God was voluntary, my brother still held the opinion that I should have been financially savvy.

Eventually, I got myself a place and then a job after a long job hunt. I still had a family that looked up to me. The job I got was great and the pay was good. However, the amount of debt that accumulated over the time I was not working was unbearable. This took me back to Grandma's advice yet again. All was starting to take shape slowly but surely.

9

The Turning Point

Being grateful was an understatement; I was happier than before. I was even planning to re-open my business as I've always wanted to be independent, being my own boss. Just like any other day, I would go to work and come back home and relax a bit before bed. I was watching TV with the family as usual, but on this occasion, it was different. I guess this was my turning point.

I dozed off as tiredness was catching up with me. I woke up hours later, and everyone else was fast asleep. I tried to reach for the remote as it was just next to the sofa. I wanted to finish the film that we had been watching. As I tried to reach for the remote, I couldn't even to stretch my hand. I tried getting up and call out but I couldn't.

At this point, I had no idea what was going on. My left side was numb. My wife, Florence, woke up to use the toilet and tried talking to me, but my speech was blurred. The good thing was that she did not panic, she called for an ambulance, and I was rushed to A&E. I was then admitted into the hospital that very same night. The doctors and nurses started running around, and at this point, I could see them, but I was in confusion.

They did all the tests and confirmed I had a stroke. As they started connecting wires all over my body, I thought this was the end of my life. My life had just flashed before my eyes. At this time, I needed God's intervention. What made it worse was when people came to visit, all I could see were the tears in their eyes.

Several questions flooded my mind; were they in mourning already? Was I dying? Were the doctors lying to me that I would be OK? I felt like I was losing all hope. The nightmare was when they took me for an Ultra-Scan. Just the sight of the machines and the noise they made would make me feel like going into a comma. During this time, I was bedridden. I couldn't bath nor use the toilet on my own. I was as good as cabbage.

I remember the most humbling part was that the Man of God came to visit me abandoning his busy schedule as I knew he would have been somewhere preaching. He turned around and said, "Your life is more important", and he prayed for me. This time my hope was restored. I then began to declare the word of God over my life according to Isaiah 53:5 (NKJV) "But He *was* wounded for our transgressions, *He was* bruised for our iniquities;
The chastisement for our peace *was* upon Him, And by His stripes we are healed."

There began THE HOLY GRIND.

A few weeks later, after going through physiotherapy, I began to see a great change. I could now use the shower on my own for the first time since the ordeal. Even someone who had hit the jackpot would not be as happy as I was. I was overwhelmed. I had just got my independence back again. I carried on with physiotherapy until the doctor came to see me after I had taken a shower unsupported.

Life in hospital was never a good thing, though, I had made friends in there of which some got out before me and others never made it out; may they rest in perfect peace. The doctor wanted to monitor my progress for a few more days, but after negotiating, he let me stay for one more day. I was so excited, and couldn't wait to get home.

10

Becoming Homeless

Through it all, the word of God was my strength. I kept confessing Jeremiah 33:6 (NKJV), "Behold, I will bring it health and healing; I will heal them and reveal to them the abundance of peace and truth." During this time, I was forced to take time off from work. As it was Agency work, I could go back at any time, but there was no income. A friend of mine came over to the house to visit me. He had a business proposal that would suit me well. I then realised no matter what I tried doing in my life; I will always go back into doing business as it's etched in my DNA.

I agreed to the proposal, and we put everything in motion. The business was familiar to me as I had acquired so many contacts within the mining sector. It required me travelling outside the country. My friend took care of the travel expenses as part of the deal. I would contact clients and set up meetings. We travelled to Africa for some minerals as our buyers were waiting for us in Dubai. We were now under pressure from our buyers as they wanted us to sign a contract worth Millions for us to supply them every month. We turned down the offer and said to them one step at a time, let's get the first delivery done then we talk.

We landed in Africa and proceeded to see our suppliers as they were already waiting for us. We got the merchandise, and all was set. The problem I then made was that I rang one of my suppliers and told him I could not see him this time around, but will come to meet him on my next visit. Hours later as I was travelling from my other supplier; we got hi-jacked, and we lost the deal.

I quickly informed the authorities, and little did I know it was the authorities that hi-jacked us as my police friend confirmed it. They would allow you to get the merchandise and hope you would pay straight away, and they hi-jack you, so they take both your merchandise and money. This was ongoing for some time, but I was not aware of it. So we decided to fly back in fear of our lives at this point as we did not know who to trust.

As I got back home, I came to the news that my wife's coughing had not stopped since I left her. She had been in the hospital for the past two weeks that I was in Africa. When I left her, she had gone to her sister's place though I knew she had a cough. I told her to get some cough remedies and other medication. It turned out to be worse than expected. So I went straight to her friend's house where she was waiting for me when she came back from her sister's.

We set down to catch up as I started to explain everything that took place and how we lost the deal. She just looked at me with tears in her eyes, and at this time, she was still coughing. So I asked her what the matter was. She gathered herself together and started to explain why she was at a friend's house instead of being at home. She told me that after she left her sister's house, she went straight home and only to find that the locks had been changed. The caretaker explained that the house owner wanted her house back and did not want to rent it out again.

They had not given us notice because initially, we didn't sign a contract or tenancy agreement with them. The owner was a friend that I had known for some time. The only thing I managed to keep was the proof of payments. I had kept all the receipts. So I went to the house to meet up the landlady to get to the bottom of the matter.

The lady explained that she had been out of the country and had no idea that someone was staying at her house. Although we were paying rent, she never received this as she left the house in the care of my friend. We then contacted the friend who claimed the lady owed him money; therefore, he put tenants in her home so that he can claim back what she owed.

She suggested we make it a police case, but I knew I had no grounds as I had no evidence or the right to be there. We left the place and managed to get a bag with our clothes and went back to my wife's friend's house. We got there and explained everything as they were like family to my wife. After explaining everything to them, they said it was a challenge for them to accommodate us as they wanted to keep their guest rooms open in case of visitors.

11

The Shelter

At this time, I was not working; my health was not 100%; my wife's health was getting even worse; it was scaring me. At this point, we had just become homeless with nowhere to go. I pleaded with the friends to consider my wife as her health was not getting any better. Being on the street would be awful for her. They only allowed us to stay a few more days and following that we were on the streets.

We moved from one shelter to another. The cold was unbearable; at times, we would just go and sit in McDonald's for shelter. I was glad that most of these food chains would be open 24/7, and they became our hiding place. I made friends with those that had been on the streets longer than me. They taught me how to grind the streets way. I remember the cold days where I would just sit in a bus stop shelter and pretend I was going somewhere and say to people, "I've just lost my bus ticket… Have you got any change?… I'm running late for an appointment."

Those moments were so humbling to think some people do this as a way of life. I felt the pain, I cried, but I realised crying would not get me anywhere. After all, what I would get from people wasn't much though but was much appreciated. At least it would get me something to eat. So much went through my mind at this time, reflecting on my life asking myself if this was it? It seemed to be one thing after another. The mistakes I had made, the wrong decisions I made along the way. But the one thing that kept me was the word of God. Jeremiah 29:11 (NKJV) says, "For I know the thoughts that I think toward you, says the Lord, thoughts of peace and not of evil, to give you a future and a hope."

I knew somehow the Lord was watching over us according to Psalms 91:14-15 (NKJV), "Because he has set his love upon Me, therefore I will deliver him; I will set him on high, because he has known My name. He shall call upon Me, and I will answer him;
I will be with him in trouble; I will deliver him and honour him."

According to David, God will protect us from dangers seen and unseen, both by day and night. Neither cruel enemies nor deadly diseases will overcome us. Just with that word in my spirit, I knew God would guard our lives as a mother bird guards her young and as a soldier guards the fortress. As I put my trust in God, I knew He would not fail me as others did. We eventually found a permanent shelter that became our home. This was more of a breakthrough. However, the challenge was that it would only open at night, and during the day it was closed.

During the day we would spend time window shopping and street grinding, and if the weather was too bad, we would just sit in McDonald's waiting for the shelter to be opened, but if you came late to the shelter, you wouldn't be allowed in; they were strict. I remember at one time, I was late, and they wouldn't allow us in, so we had to settle for McDonald's considering at the shelter we used to have our meals there and breakfast, but on this occasion, we missed everything.

The most humbling experience was during the night time as we all gathered in the hall after watching TV as a family, and we would all pray. I was truly moved by seeing my fellow homeless brothers and sisters crying out to God in prayer. That moved my heart, and that time I made a vow with God when I was out of this place, I would come back for them and even others I've not seen. I would want to make a difference in their lives. In my spirit, I knew I was not there to stay, but I believed God brought me there for a reason, to carry His burden. Matthew 25:41-43 (NKJV), "Then He will also say to those on the left hand, 'Depart from Me, you cursed, into the everlasting fire prepared for the devil and his angels: for I was hungry and you gave Me no food; I was thirsty and you gave Me no drink; I was a stranger and you did not take Me in, naked and you did not clothe Me, sick and in prison and you did not visit Me.'"

I remember at the shelter I was now known for loving rugby that they would sacrifice to watch their favourite programmes. I came to love my new family, and I knew God had put me there for a reason. Although we were all homeless, there was something different about it all. I never felt lonely; there was so much love around even though most people saw the homeless differently. The most powerful thing that I learnt from the people was that every one of them lacked the belief system that they could get out of it and be successful.

At one point, I almost fell into the same mind frame. I asked most of them how they had coped over the years, and they told me that even getting a meal was a significant challenge. I knew it had to do with their mindsets for if they had a positive mindset and a positive mentality, it would help them to turn their lives around. I never knew that at one point in my life, I would be wondering where next I would get my meals or sleep. Sitting on the bare concrete in the cold with shame and hopelessness written on my face; I could not hide my pain anymore. I spent hours crying on my own as I didn't want the rest of my roommates to see my anxiety since I had become a source of encouragement to most of them.

I wished my parents were alive maybe I would have gone home to them, but then I realised that I had a family looking up to me as a parent and the head of the household, so I had to find courage and dust myself and kept pushing and hoping for the best.

12

Waiting Upon The Lord

Homelessness isn't something that anyone should experience. It is one of the most excellent life lessons that there is. The life on the street taught me to put much life into perspective, and it made me appreciate what you have. I realised many people lived without material luxuries. My parents had always sown a seed of entrepreneurship in me, but life taught me to play it safe.

When I lost everything or instead sacrificed everything that I had worked hard for, something inside me always knew that I didn't belong where I was. To be an entrepreneur means that you will dance to a particular beat that only you can hear and no one else. That said, you have no boss, and you control your life the direction you intend for it to go than working or being under someone.

As all this resulted in me being homeless, I learned a lesson that would help me in the future as an entrepreneur. I was on my own, and my destiny was within my own hands, and the only person that could help me was the person in the mirror. There on the streets, I was my own boss. I couldn't count on others all the time; whether I chose to believe it or not, everyone had their own set of issues to deal with.

At this time, I remember I would lie to my family, especially when they would want to come to visit us. I would make up some stories that we were not around; we've travelled for a while and even change our numbers. I would convince everyone that I was fine, and everything was just fine. The only thing I had under control was my denial. It was so painful to realise that I had fallen on hard times, and the idea of sharing my pain and struggles with those that were equipped to help me was unreal.

I knew that most of them would not have believed me due to the lifestyle that the media had portrayed of me; being on TV, flying around the world, driving super cars and wearing the most expensive suits that money could buy.

One of the most pivotal moments that happened to me was that I had just been in hospital due to a stroke and had not fully recovered and my wife's health was a mess, as she wasn't getting any better. Without a source of income and consistent access to healthy food, we only ate what we could and only when we could. After a while, being at the shelter, I bumped into my previous business associate whom I had travelled with to Africa. I was doing window shopping as if I could buy anything, but it was more for time-wasting just hoping for a breakthrough.

Indeed, the breakthrough came when he invited me to stay with him until I got back on my feet. As I needed to say my goodbyes at the shelter, I agreed to visit him the next day. Saying goodbye was painful, but I promised to come back to visit even though at the back of my mind, I knew I had an assignment to care of them than just visit.

We stayed with our friends temporarily for two months. They were unbelievably kind and generous and did not make us feel like we were strangers. On the street, I would walk around the malls and housing agents for hours hoping to get a place of our own but only to be exhausted from looking at empty properties wondering if could I live there.

There's always a feeling of powerlessness when you're homeless, and you feel lost. But the Holy Grind kept me in check according to Isaiah 40:31 (NKJV) "But those who wait on the Lord Shall renew their strength; They shall mount up with wings like eagles, They shall run and not be weary, They shall walk and not faint." If you trust in your strength, you will fail, no matter how capable you may think you can. But if you believe in God, He will continuously strengthen you through his power which leads us to victory. We had been beyond all we could, hustled all we could, but it only took the word of God to strengthen us as we had used all our strength and did all that anyone could have done.

13

In Search of A Solution

I remember the nights I cried. At one time, my wife was taken to the hospital due to the coughing as we did not understand what was causing it. We got to the hospital, and at that time, she had become worse as she was now struggling to breathe properly. The doctors did all they could; rushed around, carried out blood tests, and we waited for her results to come back. Hours later, the results came back and were all clear of the tests they had ran. The doctors said she could go home and that she will be just fine if she takes medication. The senior doctor came in and said they needed to run some more tests, and we stayed overnight.

During the course of the night, I started asking God when all this would end? I realised crying wouldn't bring change. I had to pick myself up. On a normal day, I would never want to be in the hospital for any reason, but at this time, it was the best place for us. There are times I wanted to give up on life but what kept me strong and focused was my family. The thought of my family played a major part in most of my decisions at this time. If I were to give up, who would look after my family? What legacy would I leave for my kids? I wouldn't want to be remembered as the father that gave up when things were tough.

So I kept the grind alive. Time went by, and we went to different doctors in search of a solution as my wife's situation was not getting any better only to be told that it was a Chronic Asthmatic condition. That was a shock to us, considering doctors who are specialists hadn't recognised it for more than seven months of none stop coughing. Things started to get better as she finally got the proper medication, and that was a relief for us.

Life had thrown all it could to us, but the word of God says in Psalms 23:4 (NKJV), "Yea, though I walk through the valley of the shadow of death, I will fear no evil; For You are with me; Your rod and Your staff, they comfort me." It never said we would build mansions or we would stay in the valley rather it says even though we go through it, we will come out at some point. It was just a phase that we were going through, although it was painful. The question I asked myself was "What do you do when you don't know what to do?" I separated myself from people for a while and got off social media to give myself time to find myself again.

Giving up was never an option for us. At this point, we would spend most of our time in the hospital with my wife as her situation was not changing. During that time, I started looking for properties and work at the same time. It's like you had a flat tyre and decided to slash the rest of the tyres instead of getting a spare wheel and carry on with your journey of grinding. I would have given up on life on so many occasions due to disappointments and doors shut on me. Even though most of the hurdles were too high for me, the word of the Lord was my strength.

Remembering Job; he was a man who was perfect before God. A man that walked upright with the Lord and yet the devil went to seek permission to torment him. The Lord gave the go-ahead and said in Job 1: 11-12 (NKJV), "But now, stretch out Your hand and touch all that he has, and he will surely curse You to Your face! And the Lord said to Satan, Behold, all that he has is in your power; only do not lay a hand on his person. So Satan went out from the presence of the Lord." Satan was given the right to take all that Job had thinking he would curse the Lord, but he did not, instead he kept looking unto God although there was a condition for Satan not to touch his life.

The Lord says in Isaiah 43:2 (NKJV), "When you pass through the waters, I will be with you; And through the rivers, they shall not overflow you. When you walk through the fire, you shall not be burned, Nor shall the flame scorch you." As God is the Creator, He has perfect knowledge of those He created. He knows our innermost thoughts as well as our physical characteristics. Wherever we travel God is with us even in darkness or light, He is the all-seeing God.

14

Never Give Up

Trials at desolate times are an opportunity for growth so we can learn to find the light in our darkness. At this time, when all was not well, it felt as if God was not present. Little did I know He was working it out for my good. Romans 8:28 (NKJV) "And we know that in all things God works for the good of those who love him, who have been called according to his purpose." For whatever suffering we may experience, it is of a little significance compared with the Glory to be revealed on the final day of victory. At this time, it did not seem like we would come out due to the pain and suffering we were going through. There's going to be anxiety when failing, but push yourself to keep going. After all, you will never know how close you are to succeeding if you quit now.

We kept grinding and finally we found a place that we could call home with all the contracts signed this time. We had to start from ground zero. We were so grateful to our friends who stood by us through it all and like Proverbs 18:24 (NKJV) says, "One who has unreliable friends soon comes to ruin, but there is a friend who sticks closer than a brother."

People may become strong friends or strong enemies, depending on how they were treated. Words will bring a person good or ill, depending on what they mean and how they have spoken. But true friendship is not easily broken or does not make a distinction between the richer partner and poorer partner but our true friend the Lord Jesus, looked beyond all our faults and shortcomings.

The new place had so much to do, as it had no carpets or furniture. The landlord of the new property came to visit us to see how we had settled in. We sat down with her and started to explain everything we had been through on our journey to where we were at that time. After listening to our story, she was moved and was in tears as my wife just sat there coughing none stop. She then said to us you shouldn't have gone through all that you went through considering you served in the Army previously.

She began to make calls whilst we were with her and I remember she rang Legion, a charity for the Ex-forces and those still serving. She then said it was their right to house us and look after our wellbeing but at that time it never registered in my mind. All the paperwork was put in place, and we then got the full support than we could ever imagine.

During this time, I realised that the hardest times often lead to the greatest moments of our lives. Tough situations build strong people in the end. I truly believe that tough times will make you step up to the next level, and that's what makes champions.

I then realised that we were more than the challenges we were facing as character cannot be obtained in ease and quiet. But through the experience of trials and suffering, can only the soul be strengthened.

It doesn't matter how many times you get knocked down. All that matters is getting back up one more time. When you fail at something, it only means you have a shot at starting all over again. When you hit rock bottom, the only way forward is to go up. During our stay at the homeless shelter, I learnt we should never judge people for the choices they made when we don't know the options they had to choose from.

Things started taking shape now as I had started working even though I had accumulated so much debt that needed to be paid off. I kept the grind on and put a plan in place to lower the debt by the day as I knew that no matter what I did, it would still be knocking on my door.

I kept on pushing and took all the challenges that came my way and had to dig deep within myself to conquer fear so I could look after my family and never letting anyone bring me down. My wife's situation was not changing at all and at this time she had lost so much weight to the extent that her mother said to bring her daughter back home. That on its own was too much for me. I started to think about so many things such as what would happen if I didn't take her back home and something worse happened. That was a new challenge that affected me mentally.

We had been to all specialists, including private doctors, and I even rang some of the men and women of God that I knew to pray for my wife, but to not much avail. Everything seemed to be working out well except for her health; it was yet another hurdle. Many times we try so hard at something, sometimes you can be so prepared and still fail, and when all fails its painful, it causes sadness, and as I think of this ordeal, it caused disappointment.

No matter what the setback may be, how severe the failure may seem, never give up. You pick yourself up, brush it off, push forward, and move on. When you adapt, you will overcome. Never did the Lord promise that the journey would be easy. According to Psalms 23:4 (NKJV), "Yea, though I walk through the valley of the shadow of death, I will fear no evil; For You *are* with me; Your rod and Your staff, they comfort me."

The word was my comfort. I kept confessing and declaring it until it came to pass. "For the vision *is* yet for an appointed time;But at the end it will speak, and it will not lie. Though it tarries, wait for it; Because it will surely come, It will not tarry," according to Habakkuk 2:3 (NKJV). For the fulfillment of the word of the vision will not take any longer than the time God planned it. As long as there's something worth fighting for and a destiny to get to Keep Grinding. Many times people lose focus and insight into opportunities that will bring progress but never engage in those things. Most of the problems we face do not even need prayer, but they just need for us to change our environment, our circles, relationships, or even the place of worship.

There are things that God has already given us, but we take

them for granted. If you are going to put your mind and heart to change the way you do some things, I guarantee you; you will see the greatest results in your life. Remember God had already given Canaan to Israel but Israel had to fight to dominate the promised land. Life does not give you what you deserve but rather what you fight for. It takes willingness, determination, discipline and courage for you to partake of that which belongs to you. Be it in relationships or business do it with passion and your heart, Keep the Grind and allow God to connect you to the Holy Spirit that will lead and guide your every step.

After settling, I remember discussing with my wife to change our plans and accommodate the needs of the less privileged. I felt that out of it all this was what God wanted us to learn and the burden was now on us.

I remember during lunch time at work, I would sacrifice my time to be with the homeless. We would have lunch together, and I would sit with them on the pavements where they would be. At times it would be cold but that really meant nothing to me as I could relate with them. One lady came up to me and asked me if I had been sincerely homeless before. But I kept encouraging everyone that this was not the end of you as long as you believe in yourself and you are hungry and desire for change not being content with your current predicament, it will happen for you.

My secret was the word of God according to Jeremiah 30:17 (NKJV) "I will restore you to health and heal your wounds, declares the Lord. Because you are called an outcast, Zion for whom no one cares." And as David said in Psalms 121:1 (NKJV),

"I will look up to the hills were my help comes from. My help comes from the Lord which made the Heavens and the Earth." I knew that this was a grind beyond my Grandma's grind as this now became the Holy Grind.

My Grandma's message that she passed onto me was that hard work would reap benefits, both materially and spiritually, and the choices I make in life and the way I live and work would have profound consequences. Most people have lost their sense of direction and others who don't really know what they want or what matters the most to them like I had lost direction when I lost all that I had achieved due to chasing the wind fulfilling someone else's dreams.

You would then believe that material rewards define success, yet you have no sense of joy and take real pleasure in what you do. My time with the homeless people changed a lot about my perspective towards what matters in life. As you get some people that would run, suffer under unhappy situations be it in relationships or working environment. Set-ups where people are fuelled by fear of failure rather than the joy of success, where being humiliated is common, and encouragement barely exists and where individuals are interested only in their own gain and not others.

Every now and again we go through times where you feel like it's all too much or too hard, and it would really sound good if you just throw in the towel. Many times I felt like throwing in the towel even though I didn't have many sheets left to throw in. My Grandma would say, "The only sure-fire way to fail is to give up." It's not a secret that our journey was painful and uncomfortable; however, it took time and many hurdles along the way. I often was tempted to quit before reaching my goal and God-given destiny.

Many times it's the distractions around us or people. When you run into obstacles along the way, and you feel your motivation starting to fade away, some people even start to tell you, you are foolish to keep trying on something that's not working. But remember you are the visionary, you know the outcome you desire.

I faced much criticism after I left behind certain people in my life. It was unbearable as they would say, "You are going through all this because you left us…" as if my life was any better when I was with them. So I removed myself from all sorts of distractions especially from social media, as this was more of their point of access. There were times I would put all my hope, energy and faith in my goals but kept hitting the wall. Above all, I would tell myself that if I was to bring that wall down it took a little hammer at a time, so I kept confessing the word of God as my hammer.

One small effort every day towards my dreams was by exercising my faith according Matthew 17:20 (NKJV), "And Jesus said unto them, because of your unbelief; I say unto you, if you have faith as a grain of a mustard seed, you shall say unto to this mountain, be thou removed and it shall be removed and nothing shall be impossible for you." But remember faith comes by hearing and hearing by the word of God, so I had to continue to meditate on the word to make myself stronger. This definitely led to the wall coming down. "If your dreams don't scare you they aren't big enough."

In life, obstacles and failures have shown me how much I wanted something. Just remember everyone is fighting their own battles and you are not alone in this journey called life. You win some, and you lose some, but learn to pick yourself up and press on to Keep the Grind alive; even when the going gets tough.

15

Joy Comes in the Morning

My science teacher always said to me during science lessons, "You should have the aim, the brief, description of the purpose, the apparatus and the method. Then you get the results whether you meet the aim or not." At this point, my life was more of a science lesson as it fitted the description through the hurdles I had to jump, the brick walls I had to break-through, and the disappoints; the results as the aim wasn't met.

Whenever you doubt yourself worth, remember the lotus flower, although it plunges to life from beneath the mud, it does not allow the dirt that surrounds it to affect its growth and beauty. Then I remembered the word of God according to Ecclesiastes 3:1-8 (NKJV), "There is a time and season for everything and purpose under the heaven. A time to get and a time to lose; a time to keep and a time cast away..." So at this time, it was that time of the season of mourning as David said in Psalms 30:5 (KJV) "For his anger endureth but a moment; in his favour is life: weeping may endure for a night but joy comes in the morning". I knew that through it all my morning was coming.

At this time we had settled well and we then decided to relocate. The Lord told Abraham in Genesis 12:1 (KJV) "Now the Lord said unto Abraham, get thee out of thy country, and from your kindred and go to the land that I will show you and I will make you a great nation and I will bless you old and you shall be a blessing." God was precise about what Abraham should or shouldn't take, not even a shoelace.

I'm glad that even through all the pain and suffering I never took anything from anyone lest they say if it weren't for us, he would not have made it. The Lord was our source of joy. Many times we live in so much fear. Fear impacts our decision-making ability and making us risk-averse. Fear overtakes your brain, and makes it impossible to concentrate on everything even saving yourself.

Fear did cripple me at one point, preventing me from moving forward, but it had to take the word of God to move us. Many are manipulated into thinking if you leave, you won't make it, so they stay bound in fear.

Finally, we relocated, and this time we did not worry about landlords. We settled in so quick. I applied for a job transfer to the new location. We then started investing, and now we were back to my Grandma's principles of business. We then managed to find ways that would sustain us knowing that one stream of income would not be sufficient for us as I had acquired so much debt during the time I had no source of income. At the same time, I had a family to look after. The turn around was unbelievable, but we kept on working on our goals and never stopping. We even began to look for more business opportunities to invest in. We were determined to build an Empire so we could leave a legacy for our children.

Currently, we are hopeful of expanding our business, at the same time, believing that one day we will be able to give back to the community. We want to help the Homeless Institutes across the city that we may able to accommodate. We want to empower homeless people so that they can be independent once they get back on their feet through support.

James 1:12 (NKJV) says, "Blessed is the man that endures temptation and trials, for when he is tried, he shall receive the crown of life, which the Lord has promised to them that love him." Though our journey was painful, and we were often ridiculed, our characters were being continually built in God.

1 Peter 5:10 (NKJV), "But may the God of all grace, who called us to His eternal glory by Christ Jesus, after you have suffered a while, perfect, establish, strengthen, and settle *you*." Because of the hardships and the suffering we have endured as a consequence of our facing the attacks of the enemy, God will build in us a firm foundation and settle us. At this point with no shadow of doubt we could see the hand of the Lord working for our good as God wiped all our tears and restored joy back to our family.

As God says, the trials and tribulations we go through are not meant to kill us but rather to make us stronger. The word has been our pillar through it all. The journey was tough as on a normal day it would be easy to encourage someone that it will get better and it's not the end especially when it's not you on the pitch. But always remember that for you to score you have to be in the game rather than on the bench.

My wife's health had just taken another turn for the better as her Asthma was now fully under control and that was a relief for us. It felt like a burden had been lifted off our shoulders by the Grace of God. Matthew 11:28 (NKJV), "Come to Me, all *you* who labor and are heavy laden, and I will give you rest." I then realised on my own strength I could not have made it but through Christ who strengthens me, my hope of Glory, fulfilling His promise to restore us and all creation.

Christ's presence in us is the hope of Glory, and His truth is full of glorious riches. If you are going to try, go all the way otherwise don't even start. This could mean losing friends, relatives and maybe even your thinking ability. It could mean not eating for days, freezing on a park bench as I experienced. It could mean mockery at times and isolation.

Always remember that isolation is a gift. All the others are the test of your endurance, of how much you really want to do it. And with all the hurdles and obstacles I endured. If you are going to pursue something, go all the way. The journey was lonely most of the time, but above all, I kept on pushing and believing as I knew that I was never alone. Psalms 121:4 (KJV) "Indeed, he who watches over Israel will neither sleep nor slumber".

As the Lord is my protector; He won't go to sleep or let me stumble. He has never let me down; He always comes through for me, and I will forever look unto Him as my help comes from Him.

The journey will lead you straight to perfect laughter. Yes, the journey was painful and my life was filled with broken pieces, terrible choices and ugly truths; but remember it's also enriched with a major comeback, peace in my soul and it can only be the Grace of God that saved my life.

No matter what you may be facing or going through now, don't throw in the towel, don't give up and don't let fear dominate your life. If I made it and came out Victorious so can you. "Those that look unto the Lord are radiant, their faces are never covered with shame," according to Psalm 34:5 (NIV).

I'm glad we have the word of God in us, as this journey was painful and traumatising but we did overcome and came out more than conquerors as Romans 8:37 (KJV) says, "Nay, in all these things we are more than conquerors through him that loved us."

May our testimony be an encouragement to you and remember that God loves you and has a plan for your life.

Be Blessed.

About the Author

Joseph M. Kings is the founder of Reach Out Ministries (ROM). He is an Entrepreneur, Husband, Father a Motivational Speaker, and the founder of Reach Out Charity Organisation.